I0463148

www.mamarazziguides.com

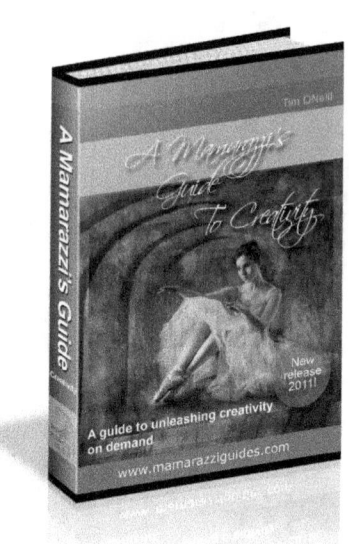

A Mamarazzi's Guide To Creativity

A guide to unleash creativity on demand

Prosperity Publishing Global

Dedication

This book is dedicated to my family.
Thank-you for being who you are and for allowing me
to be me. May God continue to bless and prosper you
all. Remember kids, readers are leaders.
Live-Love-Laugh

Mamarazzi Guides: An Introduction

Mamarazzi –noun, (plural) [mah-muh-raht-see]

(singular): (*m*) **Mamarazzo** or (*f*) **Mamarazza**) [mah-muh-raht-soh, mah-mah-raht-tsaw

What the heck is a Mamarazzi? Let me explain. Mamarazzi is derived from the term (1)paparazzi and is used by many long term Portrait Photography professionals as a negative connotation for a mom with a camera.

Since digital imaging swept the scene of image making there has been a steady increase in the number of people who become professional photographers. The demographics of this huge influx of people has primarily been women in the 22-35 age group, Moms who endear to stay at home with their new family and yet have a creative outlet and an opportunity put together an income. Personally I love this. Admittedly, I seem to be in the minority amongst other professional photographers.

Capitalism has always been my friend so I tend to see the world through glasses tinted with abundance as opposed to scarcity. The financial pie of any given industry is ever expanding and grows as more people come into the industry. The industry continues to mature and change as new fresh ideas emerge. New business comes from a renewed shared awareness of the industry or niche as a whole. Many people disagree with that assessment and believe that the pie is finite and therefore their slice is diminished with each new person coming in.

(1) *The following information came from Wikipedia at http:// en.wikipedia.org/wiki/Paparazzi#Legality_of_paparazzi*
The word "paparazzi" is an eponym originating in the 1960 film La dolce vita directed by Federico Fellini. One of the characters in the film is a news photographer named Paparazzo (played by Walter Santesso). In his book Word and Phrase Origins, Robert Hendrickson writes that Fellini took the name from an Italian dialect that describes a particularly annoying noise, that of a buzzing mosquito. In his school days, Fellini remembered a boy who was nicknamed "Paparazzo" (Mosquito), because of his fast talking and constant movements, a name Fellini later applied to the fictional character in La dolce vita. This version of the word's origin has been strongly contested. For example, in an interview with Fellini's screenwriter Ennio Flaiano, he said the name came from a southern Italy travel narrative by Victorian writer George Gissing, By the Ionian Sea. The book, published in 1901, gives the name of a hotel proprietor, Signor Paparazzo. He further states that either Fellini or Flaiano opened the book at random, saw the name, and decided to use it for the photographer.

This story is documented by a variety of Gissing scholars and in the book A Sweet and Glorious Land: Revisiting the Ionian Sea (St. Martin's Press, 2000) by John Keahey, and Pierre Coustillas.[1]

1- ^ *Pierre Coustillas, «Gissing and the Paparazzi». In : Francesco Badolato, George Gissing, romanziere del tardo periodo vittoriano; postfazione di Andrea Sciffo, Soveria Mannelli : Rubbettino Editore, 2005, ISBN 88-498-1193-4, pp. 256-266 (on-line)*

Mamarazzi guides

Mamarazzi guides are a series of books, webinars, workshops and other creative instructional material to help the new photographer rise to the level of competency to compete in the field. While there are a ton of really good books on capturing a fine image, the guides are a comprehensive look at business as a whole including business planning, traditional and web based marketing as well as the technical aspects of capturing beautiful images.

Mamarazzi guides are for those folks that think the way we think and are eager to learn. I am excited about the influx of new people to the industry and honored to be amongst the old guard who embrace the throng and not only share the knowledge gained over the years but learn from the passion and commitment newcomers to the field bring.

You can find out more about the Mamarazzi guides by visiting mamarazziguides.com.

******Men don't be afraid, the information is the same for all aspiring photographers regardless of gender.*****

★ FIND ME HERE

Twitter: http://twitter.com/tim_oneill

My Facebook profile: http://www.facebook.com/timoneill

LinkedIn:http://www.linkedin.com/in/timvoneill

Email: tim@digitalpaintmagazine.com

http://www.Mamarazziguides.com

http://www.MamarazziAcademy.com

http://www.digitalpaintmagazine.com

http://www.digitalartacademy.com

http://www.digitalpaintingforum.com

<u>Table of Contents</u>

Chapter 1
Definition of Creativity

"Creativity is…seeing something that doesn't exist already. You need to find out how you can bring it into being, and that way be a playmate with God." - Michele Shea

According to Webster's Dictionary, the definition of creativity is artistic or intellectual inventiveness. Creativity is marked by the ability or power to create or bring into existence, to invest with a new form, to produce through imaginative skill, to make or bring into existence something new. When you create something, you are actually bringing it into being, making it from nothing. But how do you make something from nothing? How do you achieve creativity? What is the essence of creativity?

Perhaps only magic can explain creativity, that sudden "aha!" moment when it all comes together. Some have said that it's something mysterious and puzzling, perhaps impossible to figure out. Some have said it must be divine inspiration. Creativity is simply thinking the impossible, and then doing what no one else has done before, sometimes developing completely new worlds. If you've taken a new approach to a problem and it works, then you're using your creativity.

Creativity comes in many forms. It can be scientific creativity, resulting in inventions or medical cures. It can be artistic or musical, resulting in beautiful paintings, sculptures or operas and songs. It can be creative writing, resulting in novels, short stories and poems. Creativity can even be as simple as arts and crafts, such as needle arts, yarn crafts, and woodcrafts - things you create with your own two hands.

The important thing to remember is that creativity includes generating the idea or concept, as well as applying that idea and producing or manifesting the end product or result. Creativity or imagination is an integral part of being human and separates us from the animal world.

> Carl R. Rogers said, "The very essence
> of the creative is its novelty, and hence
> we have no standard by which to judge
> it."

Chapter 2
Are You Creative?

"The only truly happy people are children and the creative minority." -
Jean Caldwell

Have you ever watched five-year-olds at play? They are curious and highly creative in their games. They don't know yet, what they don't know. Their creative limits have no bounds; no one has told them that they can't do something. They're fearless explorers, artists, or musicians; some are even comedians in the making. They have not yet been pressured to conform and they think they can do anything and that nothing is beyond their capabilities.

Research shows that every human being is capable of creative thought. We have creative abilities that often show up very early in life. Studies show that the average adult thinks of only three to four alternate ideas for any given situation, while the average child can come up with sixty. They have proven that as far as creativity is concerned, quantity equals quality. Having the subjects make a list of ideas, they have shown that the longer the list, the higher the quality of the final solution. The very best ideas usually appear at the end of the list.

Actually, creativity is bred into us as humans; it's in our genes - a part of our very DNA. Unfortunately, as we grow older, the pressures of having to grow up, go to school, get a job, all seem to repress our creative tendencies. The stress of everyday living, coupled with occasional dilemmas, leaves us too drained to be truly creative.

But creativity is power and is essential to our well-being. Without creativity, our lives become predictable, routine, boring, and pedantic. The good news is we can all be highly creative. Now I know you're saying, "But I'm not at all creative. I can't paint or even draw a straight line, I don't know one note from another, and I've never been able to write worth a darn. Poetry? Don't make me laugh!"

Okay, so most of us are not Mozart, DaVinci, Einstein, or Shakespeare. However, we are all creative in our own way. We simply have to recognize our own unique talents and skills. Ask yourself these questions:

1. Are you constantly looking for new goals, something new to accomplish?
2. Do you like to look at what already exists and ask "What if?"
3. When you try something new and different, does it make you feel smarter?
4. Do you enjoy teaching someone a new skill?
5. Are you good at problem solving?

Then, pat yourself on the back - you are a "creative" person! Creativity doesn't always result in a tangible product. Sometimes its ideas, problem solving, or teaching; but it is indeed, creativity in action. Creativity enables us to better ourselves, develop awareness, and expand our horizons as well as those of other people.

When the potential for creativity meets the promise of skill, you've made contact with the creative spirit. There's no holding you back now. You've received that flash of inspiration, that "aha!" moment of illumination, and you are ready to take those creative risks.

Now, you're probably wondering exactly what it is that you need to do to assure yourself of creative success. You do need certain tools and skills to accomplish this task. First, you need a certain expertise in whatever arena you've chosen to pursue your creativity in. If you have zero knowledge in the field of science, odds are you will not make the next fantastic breakthrough in medicine or invent the replacement for the wheel. You must find the field that is your special interest and skill setting. Some expertise is essential for success.

The next tool essential for your success is the ability to think creatively in your chosen field - being able to imagine a whole realm of possibilities. That includes the ability to turn things over in your mind until you find the answer. Persistence is required - that determination to keep on tackling a problem until you solve it. Know when to turn things upside down and look at them differently. You must know when to nurture the process of creativity and when to let it rest in your mind until it's ready to fly free.

Another vital tool in this search for creativity is courage - to be willing to take the creative risks and try something you've never tried before. You have to be open to whatever new possibilities that present themselves to you. You never know when ideas will come.

Finally, you must have passion - the desire to succeed no matter what. It doesn't matter what the end prize happens to be or what manner of compensation you might receive. The passion is all that's important - the desire to make whatever works, no matter what. Albert Einstein said, "Sticking to it is the genius."

Most importantly, you must face any creative risk with the mind of a child. Childhood is when creativity first comes to you. Will it grow or be stunted? You should play like a child.

Children may not realize it, but playtime is actually a learning process. It's the brain's favorite way to learn. The child learns about math, verbal skills, music, and visual arts during playtime. They learn to explore and they learn the thrill of discovery. They learn about their own culture and others as well.

So, is it true that children are more creative than adults are? During the Industrial Revolution, two hundred years ago, this country devised the educational system and started training people to be good little workers and always obey instructions. This didn't leave much room for individuality or nonconformity in our thinking. The good news is that today's educational system, for the most part, allows children to be more freethinking and creative.

Childlike creativity should be studied and emulated. Let yourself think that anything, even something outrageous, is possible. This will help you develop creative connections. The non-creative mind says, "I can't," but the creative mind says, "I can and here's how!" If you can see, speak, hear, remember and understand, you too can be creative. Never, ever say you're not creative. Whatever you believe or disbelieve about yourself, you're right.

How do you feel about being creative? Do you tie creativity to strange, artsy, or flaky behavior? Do you feel suspicious of those with that description? Or maybe you automatically tie creativity with extremes of madness or psychosis. "I'm too down to earth to be creative!" you protest.

Sometimes you are in possession of facts already known to the world at large. The difference is in your organization and interpretation of those facts. Perhaps your creativity lies in your ability to take a room full of people and convince them to make a buying decision. Maybe you've saved your company millions of dollars with a single idea. Ever resolved a conflict in your family or company? Guess what? You're creative!

Maybe you've even been told how talented you are in a particular area; you may even know it to be true. So why be shy about it? But what do you do about it? How do you go about unleashing all that talent? How do you nurture it?

Let's go back to the idea of being more childlike, unhampered by daily life and stress. Let's play! Grab a drawing pad and colored pencils, and draw circles and patterns. If you have children of your own, borrow one of their coloring books and crayons, and join them in the coloring fun. Make objects of outrageous colors, just as children do. Color outside the lines, way outside the lines! Find yourself some clay or Playdoh and start sculpting; it doesn't have to be anything in particular; just have fun with it. Squish it, cut it, slice it, and then mash in all together again. Try making shapes with the clay.

Now you're asking, "What on earth is the purpose of all that nonsense?" Well, there is no purpose, you just need to play, have fun, and be free. It's amazing how much your brain will appreciate this 'no purpose' playtime. You suddenly discover that you're more relaxed. You may even feel happy. Even your breathing rhythm is different while you're playing. Instead of the short, shallow breaths you take when you're stressed, you're now breathing deeply. You're not experiencing the 'fight or flight' sensation. You're totally relaxed. You need to push the worries and stress aside once in a while. Do not worry about problems or deadlines, and just play, with no purpose whatsoever.

Just a few minutes a day of the 'no purpose' play will make a world of difference in your creativity, problem solving, mediating, teaching, or anything else that you do. You'll soon realize it's time to take that talent to the next level, so let that creativity come out more often and let yourself go. Stephen Nachmanovitch once said, "The most potent muse of all is our own inner child."

Keep in mind though, that talent is not enough. Let me repeat this. You must have absolute passion and discipline to develop your creativity. You must be dedicated to commit to your talent.

What does the word creative make you think about? Breathtaking art? Totally original thinking? Exciting musical composition? Astonishing inventions? Have you let yourself believe that it's impossible for you to be creative?

You may have let yourself become a creature of habit over the years. Have you condemned yourself to be incapable of creative thought? Perhaps you've been stuck in a rut or boring routines, and you feel that you couldn't possibly be capable of change.

Now, imagine how your life would be if you're allowed to live it creatively, every day. You know you're creative and talented. What if the world around you treated you as such and you were allowed to nurture that talent, enhance your skills, and give your creative personality the attention it needs and deserves? You'd trust your own creative passions, be capable of solving any problem, and embrace your own creativity as a part of your very life - one of the necessary components to your happiness and mental health.

Remember that pure enjoyment is a key ingredient in your creative life.

Eileen Caddy said, "Live and work but do not forget to play, to have fun in life and really enjoy it."

Chapter 3
Integrate Creativity into Your Life

"Leap and the net will appear." Julia Cameron

Okay, we've established the fact that everyone is basically creative. You've recognized the creative energy that you possess; and that creative energy must go somewhere or be applied to something, or you will find yourself unhappy and unfulfilled, without understanding exactly why.

The benefits of adding this creativity to your everyday life are numerous:

1. Self-confidence
2. Reduced stress
3. Inner peace
4. Better control of your life
5. Unbelievable satisfaction at last
6. You're expressing yourself
7. Finding purpose.

By applying this creativity to all aspects of your life, you'll discover even more benefits.

So, how do you apply your creative energy to your daily life? You apply that newly discovered creativity to family and relationships, to work, and to your community. It's time to explore all the possibilities and perhaps better our world. Simply start with your own little corner of it. You must implement those marvelous new ideas to your information gathering and problem solving. Create checklists and plans. Adapt a new idea; give it a twist. Allowing your creative side to show can make you more competitive in the corporate world. You can look at something that everyone else has looked at, but see it in a totally different light. Give it that twist. Go with that hunch, that intuition, that special insight the creative person possesses. "A hunch is creativity trying to tell you something," said Frank Capra. Those little creative moments are vital to every area of your life.

Once you start on this creative journey, you'll discover that your life is filled with the "aha!" moments. Push beyond the mere routine and let yourself come up with dazzling visions or earth-shaking ideas.

Webster's Dictionary defines innovation as the introduction of something new or different. The National Innovation Initiative (NII) defines innovation as "The intersection of invention and insight, leading to the creation of social and economic value." So take that creativity and let yourself be innovative!

Jack London once said, "You can't wait for inspiration, you have to go after it with a club." If you need to come up with new ideas, say for work, try brainstorming. You can do this alone or with others. This works especially well in the work environment. Many hands make light work, and many minds make marvelous new and unique ideas. It also makes for a convivial work place. Just let your mind go wherever it needs to go.

Then you must act on your creative impulse. Without action behind it, it's only just so many facts, a little knowledge.

> *Albert Einstein said, "Creativity is more powerful than knowledge."*

Chapter 4
Creativity in the Work Place

"Creative minds have always been known to survive any kind of bad training." - Anna Freud

In today's competitive world, it is more important than ever for businesses to attract and keep highly talented people. In order to do that, they must provide a work place environment that is challenging, creative, and fun. Since creativity is at the root of innovation and invention, it would behoove all companies - large, small, or in between - to help promote a creative atmosphere in which this talent may flourish. What better way to get a huge return on their investment?

A two-year in-house creativity course offered at General Electric resulted in a sixty percent increase in concepts available for patents, according to the Wall Street Journal.

In 1999, after investing over two million dollars in research and development, Hewlett Packard generated more than 1,300 applications for patents.

When the Sylvania Company offered several thousand employees a forty-hour creative problem-solving course, their return on investment came to $20 for every $1 they spent.

So how can your company keep its employees happily coming up with great, innovative ideas?

- Look for these creative people. Recognize them for the intelligent innovators that they are.

- Create an atmosphere that's conducive to creativity. You need to let the ideas come forth and thrive. Be tolerant about ideas that don't work out initially. There's always a next time when more fresh ideas can be implemented.

- Acknowledge the people in the company who generate new ideas. It's important to foster that creativity and show visible support. Champion those innovators!

- Reward the creators with public recognition, monetary rewards, or both.

The workers and the managers should bring about creative changes in the company together, shaping a fellowship that allows for a feeling of safety for those creative ideas. It should provide an environment where people can feel secure about expressing those ideas, without being fearful of criticism or ridicule.

The feelings of respect and trust for one another will foster inspiration, and dismiss any negativity or critical judgments. The perfect atmosphere would be one of encouragement, motivation, good training, and lots of opportunities to be creative. This would provide the necessary creativity to the organizational level.

No longer would you go to a work place that fills you with dread each day. The job that provides you with money for food, clothing, and shelter, not to mention a few luxuries, could also be a pleasant haven during the workday. You'd have security and status, but without so much stress. If your creativity is allowed to blossom, your heart and soul for your career returns as well. This could change the face of the work place. Implement this yourself and see if you can make a change for the better in your own workplace.

Many companies try to avoid putting creativity back into the work place. They feel it could lead to chaos. They say that it would be illogical, unruly, and uncontrollable. This needn't be the case, if approached in the proper manner.

If you encourage creativity within your company and support the talented people, it will help you compete, regardless of your industry. According to Fortune Magazine (January 1998), highly motivated employees are up to 127% more productive than those averagely motivated employees in complex jobs. It's simple - if an employee feels satisfied and encouraged in his job and happy with the company, he will become more motivated and thereby become more productive. A happy worker is a productive worker!

Unfortunately, our country has become a nation of workaholics. We feel if we're not busy 24/7, we must be slacking off; we must produce nonstop or other people will think that we're lazy. But busyness for its own sake is a sign of low self-worth and should be avoided. Even God rested after working for six days.

It's okay to sit and do nothing once in a while. Sometimes, you have to let a problem sit awhile and incubate in your mind. The answer will come more easily if you stop obsessing about it. Even daydreaming is useful. If you allow your child to daydream, they will develop a higher IQ. Why not do the same for yourself? Remember too, that play is just as important for an adult as it is for a child.

Believe it or not, the number one concern of employees at any level of a company is not money, but the desire for a good balance between their work life and their personal life. In order for good employees to keep up with the level expected of them, they must attain a certain balance of work and play. Vacations, occasional personal time, and a pleasant work place are essential for their careers and their health.

There's a Zen saying that the bow kept forever taut will break. This is very true. We need to play and relax in order to be productive. Play, even at our work place, makes us happy and joyful. It clears those cobwebs out of the brain and allows us to think more clearly, thus becoming more productive. The problems that seemed beyond your reach while brainstorming might come so much easier when your mind is free of stress and worry.

Creativity and play are essential these days. We're all looking for more purpose in our lives, and we're beginning to re-think our jobs and careers as well. Job security is a thing of the past; and unless employers begin to recognize and encourage creativity on the job, there could be radical changes coming.

In many companies, smart employers are beginning to see the advantage of closely-knit teams working together to form creative, problem-solving forces. They've begun using a more open kind of office, omitting walls between the departments. They're making use of more computers and other forms of communication with each other. Department heads are working more closely with the lower levels, so they are aware of what's happening at all times. The chain of command is made simpler, responsibilities are expanded, and creative and innovative ideas are welcomed and encouraged.

In any job or profession, there are problems to be solved; and where there is problem solving, there will be creative thought. The first step to solving a problem is to know everything you can possibly know about the problem. You must know how it started and what caused it. Get hold of all pertinent information.

Start to look at all the facts. Figure out how they fit together. Sometimes, you'll find that unlikely elements can start to make some sense together. Try not to fall into what scientists jokingly refer to as "psycho sclerosis" or hardening of the attitudes. This just means not falling back into the "this is the way we've always done it" syndrome. If it has always been done that way, why is there a problem with it now? Obviously, it isn't working now, so it's time to figure out a new way to do things.

Watch out for the notorious "inner critic." (More about that in another chapter.) This is simply that little voice in your head that tells you it's impossible for you to solve this problem. It's the old "if others haven't been able to solve this muddle, what makes you think you can?" critic. Disregard this voice. Unfortunately, you might also hear this selfsame voice coming from others as well. Remember the words of Mark Twain, who said, "The man with a new idea is a crank until the idea succeeds."

Watch out too for the frustration that can come at you. Long hours of preparation and anguish, when the answer doesn't present itself, can often lead to total frustration with the whole project. You just want to throw up your hands and yell, "I quit!" But don't! That's just the "darkness before the dawn," as they say. Stay persistent. The answer is out there and you'll find it; just don't give up. It's not that a problem is unsolvable; sometimes, people just give up too quickly.

Sometimes, you just have to let that thought simmer in your brain for a while, let things gel a bit. Maybe you just need to "sleep on it." Let your subconscious work on it for the night. (More on the subconscious in another chapter.)

Often times, going on about your usual business, getting ready for work, showering, and shaving will break the dam and the brilliant ideas just pop to the surface of your brain. A long walk or a drive in the country will make all the difference. You just need to relax and let those ideas simmer in your brain until they're done. Maybe it's time to play!

Try to take a break often during your day and let your mind rest a bit. Our world is encroaching on our thinking time, all during the day. Your boss, associates, teachers, students, even television, all want to tell you what you should be doing, every minute of the day. Sometimes, you just need a break from all the mind controlling going on and think your own thoughts.

Whether it's on the job or at home with your family, the creativity you possess is a vital tool in your life. Have faith in your own creativity. Don't be so hard on yourself if things don't work the first time. Be an observant human, watch everything, learn, and don't be afraid to ask the dumb questions. You know what they say - the only dumb question is the one you didn't ask.

Chapter 5
Nurturing the Creativity Within

"An idea can turn to dust or magic,
depending on the talent that rubs
against it." - Bill Bernbach

Now that you've accepted the fact that you are indeed a creative person, and that you are capable of becoming creative more than you have ever dreamed of, it's time to put that talent to work and practice, practice, practice.

The first thing you need is a place in which to be creative - a space of your own. If possible, it should be a space that's comfortable and conducive to creative thinking - a place free of distraction and noise.

To start with, you will need a desk, a comfortable chair, good lighting and the proper tools or equipment. At this stage, you are only focusing on your creativity and formulating ideas. You're still brainstorming. To help you focus, you might try a little mood music.

Grab that pen/pencil and paper. If you like, you can use a recorder. Whatever medium you choose, make sure you record every single idea; don't let any of them get away. You may not be able to retrieve them later. At this stage, don't try to censor yourself, just write down everything that occurs to you, no matter how silly or bizarre it might sound.

Don't be negative; this is no time to be critical with yourself. Just let yourself go. Try writing for about fifteen minutes at a time. Natalie Goldberg says to just keep your hand moving across the page. Francis Bacon said, "Write down the thoughts of the moment. Those that come unsought for are commonly the most valuable." Then take a break. Get up, stretch, take a walk, and relax

Give yourself time every day to daydream, to ask "What if?" Remind yourself you're a creative being and allow yourself to maintain that childlike wonderment. Question everything. When you run into the "That's just the way we've always done things," attitude, try this:

- Ask why.
- Think of a new way to do things. Think outside the box, as they say. Don't be afraid to challenge traditional thinking.
- Maintain the motivation.
- When something strikes you as interesting, go with it and find the twist.

Keeping a journal is an excellent way to avoid losing all those marvelous ideas your creative mind is capable of churning out. Allow yourself that spontaneous creativity.

Increasing the creativity in your life is easy if the activities you've chosen are of particular interest to you. William Shakespeare said, "No profit grows where is no pleasure taken, in short, study what thou dost affect." Simply put, do what you love and you will succeed. You work hardest where your heart lies.

Give yourself the proper incentive to work hard on developing your creativity. Don't wait for inspiration to strike. Sit down and begin the process of creating; and the Muse, in curiosity, will appear.

Many times, visualization is very helpful in the process of creating a new idea. Each person has their own way to bring their creativity to the forefront. You will doubtless find your own way to entice the Muse to visit you. Benjamin Franklin used to take air baths to stimulate his thinking. The ritual itself is not important; it's only a way of focusing your mind on developing creative ideas. Other factors may include a music that inspires you, the time of day when your creativity is at peak, or working in a particular place each time. The important part is to train your mind to think creatively. This takes a little time and effort, but is well worth it in the long run. When creative inclinations (such as questioning everything, asking what if, and stretching your mind) become automatic, you can pat yourself on the back. You're developing the creative side of your brain, inviting the Muse. Congratulations!

Remember, developing creative ideas is not enough. You must back it up with action

> *. Robert Ringer said, "Nothing happens until something moves." Put those wonderful ideas into motion.*

Take action!

Chapter 6.
Oops! It's Okay to Make Mistakes

"To live a creative life, we must lose our fear of being wrong." - Joseph Chilton Pearce

One of the biggest reasons why you might not nurture your creative side is fear - fear of making a mistake, fear of not getting something exactly right, fear, fear, and more fear. "What if I mess up?" "What if people laugh at me?" "What if this is just a foolish notion?" Unfortunately, that is going to happen. Everybody fails sometimes; but it's okay. Failure isn't fatal or permanent. Even Thomas Edison had some failures and it took him many trials before he perfected the light bulb. He didn't consider them as failures; however, he just found many great ways that didn't work. But he persevered and eventually, he succeeded.

Never fear making mistakes. Remember that perfectionism is a deterrent to your creativity. (More on that in a later chapter.) Albert Einstein noted "A person who never made a mistake never tried anything new." Don't let fear keep you from being creative. You won't learn as much from winning as you will from losing. Your mistakes teach you much more than your triumphs do.

The upside of not succeeding right away is that we often encounter the magical "serendipity." Serendipity is the ability to make unexpected and fortunate discoveries. It is simply accidental good fortune. What you fear to be a dreadful mistake might instead turn out to be the perfect answer to the problem.

Do insights come suddenly or are they in your subconscious, just waiting to leap upon the stage of your consciousness? That's hard to say. You might call it mere chance, coincidence, pure randomness, or complete unpredictability. How the creative thought gets to you is not the issue. Seizing upon the new idea is what's important.

Sometimes, you need to go outside the box in your thinking. Do something completely different. The definition of insanity is doing the same thing repeatedly the same way, but expecting a different outcome. That's where creative thinking comes in. Think of the same problem, but in a different way. Turn it on its side, or on its head. Look at the whole thing from different angles. Take an entirely different approach to the question. Oliver Wendell Holmes taught us "Man's mind stretched to a new idea, never goes back to its original dimensions." Thank goodness for that!

For many, the 'out-of-the-box' thinking is difficult and strange. Human beings are creatures of habit and tend to do things as they've always been done, exactly how they've always been taught to do something. Unfortunately, this is very restrictive, non-creative thinking. Do you sometimes feel like the mime inside the glass box? Trapped inside and always trying to figure a way out? Try finding a creative solution to your escape. Perhaps a special key or maybe just a large hammer would do the trick.

Scott Adams said, "Creativity is allowing yourself to make mistakes. Art is knowing which ones to keep."

Chapter 7
Enemies of Creativity

"We may encounter many defeats, but we must not be defeated." - Maya Angelou

As promised in a previous chapter, it's time to discuss the dreaded "enemies" of your creativity. Anything that stops the natural flow of creativity is known as a block. There are many different reasons they occur and it requires some work on your part to re-establish that creative flow.

There are several thieves of your creative time. These are the blocks to your creative thoughts and ideas. But don't be afraid; while they may seem daunting, you can learn the process of deflecting them.

Sometimes, daily life itself is the thief of your creative time. Perhaps you worry about caring for your children, or even elderly parents. If your day job is time-consuming or boring, you might dream of time to just let your imagination go where it wants. Ill health might also be your greatest worry and time stealer.

Here's the first place to let your imagination take over and help you find that creative time you need. Creativity over your daily life is your first challenge. All you need to begin with is a few minutes to yourself. Use your journal to record the problems you face and practice coming up with some creative ways to work through them.

The hardest part is learning to focus on one challenge at a time, giving it your conscious and subconscious attention. If your life is very stressful, that just means you need the creative time more than ever. You must give to yourself, or you'll have nothing to give others in your life. Dr. Phil McGraw said, "You can't give from an empty cup."

I can hear you right now saying, "When can I possibly find time to be alone and think about anything but my problems. There's so much to do, so much to accomplish, and not nearly enough time to do them all. Where do I fit in time for myself?"

If you come home from a long day of work, and then have small children demanding your time, it's actually a perfect time for a little creativity. Playtime with them in the form of coloring, playing with clay, and reading are ideal ways to exercise your own creativity. They are also great ways to relax. The benefits to the children are that you are helping to build their self-esteem and self-confidence. Children love doing things with their parents. Praise them lavishly to help boost their own creativity and self-worth. If you're responsible for older people, try some board games, card games, or hobbies to connect with them and spur on your own creative forces, as well as theirs.

Then give yourself a few minutes before bed to sit quietly and think your own creative thoughts. Meditation is an excellent way to teach your mind to focus and concentrate on your own creativity. When you go back to your journal, you may be pleasantly surprised at how successfully and creatively you've solved any problems you've faced. Making meditation a part of your day could make all the difference in your mood and your health.

You've discovered that being busy, and yet finding creativity in your life, is very possible. But there are other obstacles you may have to face. Sometimes you may find that you have conflicting goals, or have not positively defined those goals. You might have a great deal of competition at work, and you might be confused as to how to take advantage of opportunities you feel are necessary to your career advancement.

Here's yet another opportunity to put your creativity to the challenge. As with any problem, you must first define it precisely. You cannot progress forward without knowing exactly what it is you want. Once you've defined the goal, it's time to set out the steps to attaining that goal. What do you need to get from Point A to Point B? You need a plan. Here's where your creativity can help you again. Make your plan, deciding how to get what you want, step-by-step, complete with a time line if necessary. Then follow your plan.

Zig Ziglar said, "You can't hit a target you cannot see and you cannot see a target you do not have." It's essential to have a plan in mind, a goal to achieve, a road map to what you want. In the absence of clearly defined goals, we become strangely loyal to performing daily acts of trivia.

Without a definite goal in mind for your life and your creativity, you may find yourself going along with someone else's plan that's not necessarily the right one for you. Go with your own creativity and find what's right for you personally.

Yet another enemy of your creativity is anxiety. It's hard to focus on brilliant ideas if you're feeling anxious. And while anxiety is not the ideal place in which to work your creative magic, it can be used to your advantage at times. Oscar Wilde said, "The anxiety is unbearable. I only hope it lasts forever." You can use that anxiety to spur you forward and keep you moving.

Other obstacles you may encounter are lack of self-confidence or fear of criticism. You must remind yourself that you are a highly creative person. Take steps to learn what you need to know to develop that creativity and your self-confidence. As for criticism, you must learn to let it roll off your back. There will always be critics in your life, and you must learn the art of ignoring them.

You may even be a bit self-critical concerning your own abilities. That inner critic is the worst of all of them, because that's the one you hear all the time. This is the voice in your ear saying, "What makes you think you can come up with the creative answer to this problem? Who do you think you are anyway?" It takes some practice to learn to turn off the inner critic when you're in the middle of creating something, but it's important that you do.

Procrastination is one of the worst blocks to your creativity. "As soon as I get some extra time, I'll get to that creative project." "I'll tackle that new project this weekend, after work." "As soon as school is back in and the kids are out of the way, I'll get to that special project."

You know you've done exactly that; you've procrastinated day after day, week after week, month after month. Yet you never seem to get around to that special project. Sometimes, you can actually use one of these enemies of creativity to inspire you. The well-known "Round Tuit" is just such an innovation. It's a yellow circular piece of rubber, stamped with "Round Tuit" on one side. At one time, it was "the thing" to give to your procrastinating friends. They're always waiting until they got around to it; well now they had one.

That creative project, that hint of a brilliant idea, that nugget of creativity continues to sit at the edge of your mind, mocking you, calling to you. It's so close, you can almost touch it. You can almost get your hands on it. But it stubbornly stays just out of reach. It taunts you, "Leave all that other stuff and come be creative with me!"

Procrastination is one of the hardest blocks to dispense with, because it feels like a legitimate excuse. After all, you're so busy, you got so much to do, and so many people depend on you and demand your time. It's so easy to keep putting it off, until you never get to it at all.

There are many types of procrastinators. There are those who wait until the last minute and tell themselves that they work better under pressure. Pressure or no pressure, they still don't accomplish anything.

There are those who either fear failure or perhaps fear success, so they avoid the project. This group would rather be thought of as lazy than without the necessary ability to accomplish the goal.

It just feels like you're being pushed, and no one likes being pushed to do anything. Trouble is, you just don't feel thrilled about doing whatever the project is. So, you avoid it as long as you can, giving excuse after excuse.

Finally, there are those who simply cannot make a decision, thinking erroneously that if they make no decision, they're not responsible.

The last block that is so difficult to deal with is that of perfectionism. You're never satisfied with what you accomplish - it's never quite right, it's not "perfect," others may not like it, etc. Many writers experience this syndrome. They write a few pages, then start the editing process, thinking it will be easier than if they waited until the story or book was finished. The problem with that theory is that you will never get past those first few pages. You are always stuck in the editing process and you will never finish at all.

Many people get so stuck in the "perfection" rut, they eventually give up the project altogether. Their reasoning is that if they can't get it just right, why bother finishing it? This is positively destructive to the creative process.

Since there is no such thing as perfection, then striving for it is a useless pursuit and a waste of your creative time. There are cultures and groups around the world who remind themselves of their own imperfection by deliberately including a flaw in their art. The Japanese call it a "wabi." Amish quilt makers always include a deliberate flaw in their work, to remind themselves that men and women are not perfect.

In this case, we must return to the childlike model of creativity. Children don't care if they get something perfect, they just love doing it. They just keep on trying, regardless of how many times they fail to achieve perfection. Remember the time when you were a child and failed to accomplish something to everyone's satisfaction. "Just do your best," your mother told you. "All you can do is your best."

"There is no failure, except in no longer trying; no defeat, except from within; no insurmountable barrier, except our own inherent weakness of purpose." – Anonymous

Chapter 8
Creativity - The First Cousin to Genius

"Genius knows where the questions are hidden." Mason Cooley

What exactly is the difference between the mind of a genius and the mind of an ordinary person? Michael Michalko, in his book **Cracking Creativity**, says he thinks the difference is that geniuses know "how" to think, instead of "what" to think. This enables them to create completely new concepts and say to themselves that anything is possible.

That simply means that they look at problems differently. They combine ideas, images, and thoughts in a different way and are able to recognize patterns in the world around them. They know how to make connections between objects, no matter how unusual or disparate. An example of this is when Leonardo DaVinci made the connection between the tone of a bell and a flat stone hitting the water, causing waves. His connection was that sound also traveled in waves.

Another sign of genius is the ability to think in opposites. An example of this type of thought would be the Danish physicist Niel Bohr. In 1928, he announced that it was possible to imagine light as both waves and particles, not however simultaneously.

The ability to think in metaphors is considered a sign of genius. Aristotle felt that if a person has the ability to compare two separate areas of existence and somehow find a relationship there, then that person has a special gift.

A person of exceptional abilities also focuses on how to analyze the process of accidental creativity. It's not a matter of why it failed, but what exactly did it do?

A person possessing genius is highly productive. An example of this was Thomas Edison, who held over 1,000 patents. In his book **Cracking Creativity**,

Michael Michalko states that geniuses produce large quantities of ideas because they think fluently. Apparently, their minds are extremely busy; they think all the time. And it's possible for the rest of us to develop these attributes as well. It's simply a matter of training our brains to think more fluently.

According to Buckminster Fuller, "Everyone is born a genius. Society degeniuses them." Some believe that genius just appears, out of the blue, and that the conditioned thinking of higher education can actually detract from a person's genius. Massive amounts of knowledge doesn't necessarily guarantee genius; it only means you have an excellent memory. And the good news is that you need not be a genius in order to be creative. And even better news is that we are capable of more than just creative thought; we are capable of more genius than we ever dreamed.

Charles Baudelaire described genius as "no more than childhood recaptured at will."

So, how do you accomplish this feat? You must retrain your brain to think like a genius. You can do that by following the above criteria. You must start to think about the world around you differently. Think in opposites, think in metaphors, and become more productive with your thoughts. And when ideas don't exactly pan out the way you hoped they would, you must ask yourself not why it failed, but what did it accomplish, what did it prove?

Want to develop the mind of an inventor? Start looking at designs around you and ask yourself how you could make them different. Max Planck, known as the father of quantum theory, believed that it was necessary for scientists to have "a vivid intuitive imagination, for new ideas are not generated by deduction, but by artistically creative imagination." Even Einstein said his theories were "free invention of the imagination."

Ezra Pound said, "Genius…is the capacity to see ten things where the ordinary man sees one and where the man of talent sees two or three, plus the ability to register that multiple perception in the material of his art."

Chapter 9
Left Brain, Right Brain

"The chief function of your body is to carry your brain around." - Thomas Edison

There is an old joke that says if the left half of the brain is dominant in right-handed people and the right half is dominant in left-handed people, then left-handed people are the only ones in their right minds.

In the late 1960s, Roger Sperry published the theory that the left half of the brain was the analytical, verbal side and the right half of the brain was the creative, visual side. Between the two halves is the corpus callosum, the connector. Simply put, the two halves communicate with each other through this connector. It's the corpus callosum that quite literally keeps the right hand informed of what the left hand is doing.

Each half of the brain receives information in a completely different way. The left half of the brain is the speech center, where you get the ability to form thoughts and put them into words. This is also where things are put into certain sequential or logical order.

The right half of the brain controls motor skills, intuition, and emotion. It also enables you to be able to recognize and identify images. While the left side thinks in words, the right side sees pictures.

Creative individuals such as artists, writers, or musicians often refer to this a dual nature.

It is possible however to shift from one side to another, making use of both sides. A human being will make the shift depending on the situation in which he finds himself to be in. Picture an accountant, who makes his living working with numbers: rows and rows, column after column of numbers. Obviously, his livelihood depends on his utilization of the left side of his brain to good effect. However, if he wants to go dancing in the evening with his wife, he must shift over to the right side of the brain - to the creative side

- the side that makes it possible for him to know how to dance.

On the other side of the coin, is the artist, who makes his living by painting beautiful landscapes or portraits. All day long, he paints, displaying his talent in vibrant colors, lights, and shadows. In the evening, he must pay his bills and balance his checkbook. So you see the shift from the right side of his brain, wherein lies his creativity, over to the left side of his brain, wherein lies his logical and analytical thinking.

Most humans are born with one tendency or the other, with influence coming from genetic traits, type of family life, and childhood training. There are exceptions, however. And change is possible; either side can be trained and strengthened.

One of the most famous examples of this type of change is the story of Theodore Roosevelt, the twenty-sixth President of the United States. As a young boy, he suffered from asthma and was ill much of the time. In order to build up his body, his father had a gym built, where Theodore could work out and overcome the weakness in his body. Later, he became a lawyer and quite a prolific writer of history and philosophy. Here is proof that a person can shift from one side of the brain to the other, depending on their circumstances.

Whatever side of the brain you prefer, will dictate your likes and dislikes, and will determine your skills, talents, and weaknesses. It will also affect your work and personal life, determining what you do for a living and who you choose to have in your life.

You may notice that changes in your life can have a definite impact on which half of the brain you use most. Shifting lifestyles and responsibilities bring about a shift in the way you see things and react to the changes. So no matter which side you prefer, you still use both sides of your brain and will find the need to shift back and forth, depending on the demand of the moment.

Let's break down the delineation of the two halves of the brain more completely. The left half of the brain controls the logical, analytical, sequential, rational, linear, verbal, goal-oriented side of your nature. The right half of the brain controls the intuitive, spontaneous, emotional, visual, artistic, playful, non-verbal side of your nature.

Right-brained people are easy to spot. They daydream, doodle, and maybe draw. They may decide, at the spur of the moment, to take a walk to nowhere in particular. They may be more aware of colors, scents, and aromas and more able to visualize scenarios, most notably the "what if" moments. They are more aware of their emotions, as well as the emotions of those around them. They relate to others more easily, understanding their point of view and experiences. Simply put, they're more intuitive and spontaneous.

Left-brained people are always asking questions and wanting answers to everything. They tend to be list makers and planners. Their idea of fun may include working on crossword puzzles and/or solving math problems. They prefer writing and outlining to spontaneous outbursts of activity. They're also more connected to time and schedules, and love to plan everything down to the last detail. They're more analytical and like to break problems down into the component parts.

Everything you do, everything you think, everything you feel, and everything you experience are directed through your brain, and filtered through the left and/or the right side.

Every human has the same basic equipment to use and draw on for life as Albert Einstein, Louis Pasteur, Leonardo DaVinci or Helen Keller. It's not the size of the brain that's important; it's what you do with yours that counts. The biggest difference in our brains and those of so-called geniuses is that they are able to make the shifts back and forth more easily and are more inclined to use both sides of their brain to the best effect.

So, how do you train your brain to be more effective? There are a few exercises to help your brain perform the shifts necessary to comprehend the world around you and effectively deal with whatever circumstances you may find yourself into over the course of your life.

One such exercise is something very simple. As children, you probably played around with optical illusions. You see one picture clearly, but if you look closely, another image appears. The once popular Seeing Eye images are good examples of optical illusions. The dual images cause your brain to shift back and forth.

Another good exercise to train your brain is good old-fashioned brainstorming. Here you must define the problem, lay it out in details, and ask yourself what you really want to accomplish. Then break the problem down into its basic components. Smaller pieces are not intimidating and are easier to deal with. If it's required, seek expert assistance when necessary. Then visualize the perfect outcome. How do you see it unfolding in your mind? Make it a pleasing outcome - the perfect solution.

Within the problem-solving exercise, you'll find yet another set to help you not only solve problems, but to help you visualize and develop your creativity.

1. Try seeing the exact opposite of your problem. Not enough workers at the office? Try picturing masses moving around.
2. Expect the unexpected.
3. Forget everything you know about the problem and start from scratch. This clears the mind of preconceived notions and allows you to see the problem, and possibly the solution, more clearly.
4. Role-play with those people involved in the problem. See their point of view. Pretend you are them.

The last exercise we'll discuss is called cinematics or seeing pictures in your mind's eye.

Sometimes, you'll experience flashbacks in your memory and see things anew - things that happened in the past. It may be an emotional experience, good or bad. You'll notice some things you remember and others you've forgotten. Holes in the memories are normal for most people.

At other times, you may want to fast forward to what you desire to happen - the perfect scenario. This is also known as "daydreaming." You've probably had

an experience where you've been admonished by teachers, parents, and other authority figures to stop daydreaming and get to work. In this case, it is altogether necessary to do some serious daydreaming. It's actually good for you and your brain, and is a great creative tool.

You will discover too, that men and women react differently to the information filtered through their right brains and left brains. Women tend to react more generally, while men react more laterally. Men tend to use their left brain and react more single-mindedly to a given situation. They proceed in a logical manner, taking one task at a time. Women are more multitasking by nature. Scientists think this comes down from primitive times, when women were responsible for cooking, cleaning, washing, and keeping the children from wandering away and being eaten by wolves. Primitive men were the hunters, requiring more single-mindedness for the hunt. Women tend to be more emotional and want to talk

about their feelings, while men repress those feelings and retreat to their addictions, like football and television. At the same time, men may get angry in a situation, which obviously calls for another reaction, and women become the mediators.

Whether it's the right brain or the left brain, it needs closure. Compared to a missing piece of puzzle, your left brain will try to find the missing equation while your right brain will find the missing image needed to solve the problem.

From a BBC documentary: Another discovery was made recently after studying those with autism and dementia. Scientists believe they have found a part of the brain, that when switched off, can stimulate artistic genius. One of the scientists, an Australian, sees a time in the future when even ordinary people will be able to hit a switch and find their own genius.

If you'd like to see whether you're controlled more by the right brain or the left brain, go to

http://www.web-us.com/brain/LRBrain.html.

There is a short quiz to help you determine which side of your brain is more dominant over the other.

Humor is also something that you can develop using both sides of your brain. Your right brain may automatically look for the humor in a funny situation, while your left brain will analyze each step in the process, determining exactly why it's so amusing.

Those controlled strongly by the left brain may feel compelled to tell you exactly why it isn't amusing as well. In this instance, it might be best to let your creative side have its way and just enjoy the moment and the humor. Keep in mind that most of the great geniuses of recorded history had excellent sense of humor.

In addition to the two sides of the brain, you also possess a screening device, a filter, if you will, located at the base of your brain called a Reticular Activating System or RAS. This is made up of a group of cells that help you decide what you're conscious of, meanwhile filtering out other kinds of unimportant information, allowing only vital input into your awareness.

If you have to acknowledge each sound, sensation, color, feeling, etc., you'd no doubt go crazy. That's just too much sensory information flooding your consciousness, every minute of every day. Yet you can access that information if you so desire, shifting your focus so that you're conscious of that less vital information, if you need it.

An example of this shift would be a new mother. Although she is able to sleep, she hears the slightest noise from the nursery. She accesses that extra information because it becomes necessary for her to have it.

If you keep your mind open to new ideas, your Reticular Activating System will allow necessary information to get through to your consciousness, giving you a whole world of inspiration.

It's also been discovered that the brain is capable of enormous recall of information. Everything you've

ever read, everything you've ever heard, and everything you've ever seen and experienced, are stored in your brain. The trouble most of us have is finding a way to access all that wonderful information.

Through meditation and sometimes hypnosis, that information can be retrieved. Meditation can strengthen the connection between the conscious and the subconscious and help the RAS to access all the stored information.

Hypnosis can often be used to take the subject back to the time they first learned some important fact or topic and reawaken that memory, bringing it to the surface, and therefore making it more accessible. You may be thinking, "Hypnosis? Isn't that a little extreme? That's too much like a parlor trick for me."

Hypnosis is simply daydreaming, so your conscious mind calms down and steps out of the way. Then your subconscious can take over temporarily. But you're still completely aware of everything that's going on around you. Your senses are merely

heightened. Your subconscious mind now has access to all the information your mind possesses and has free rein to use it all.

The good news is that you can do this yourself; no hypnotist is needed. You just need to learn to daydream to your best effect. By giving your subconscious access to your memories and information, it will also be able to tap into your creative side - to make connections and find relationships between ideas that your conscious mind might just filter out.

Exercising your mind is often helpful in accessing information. Albert Einstein, when faced with a problem, would walk away for a few minutes, and play his violin. Upon returning to the original idea, he's often presented with a solution to the problem. Leaving the dilemma for a while, taking a walk, or listening to music, often helps immeasurably in relaxing your mind, so it can solve the problem. This is the subconscious moving forward again and aiding in problem solving.

Your brain is also capable of multitasking. Watch any stay-at-home mom, as she cooks dinner, feeds the baby, talks to her friend on the phone, breaks up a fight between the two older children, and answers the front door to deal with a salesman.

Her constantly busy senses are sending feedback to her brain, insuring that all the tasks get completed. Without her conscious effort, her lungs process oxygen, her heart pumps blood, and her temperature is maintained. She gets the dinner, finishes feeding the baby and puts him down, ends her conversation and hangs up the phone, sends the two little fighters to their opposite corners, and sends the salesman on his way.

Thanks to our subconscious, we can drive a car, play a piano, or watch television and still talk to friends at the same time.

The brain processes information every second, of every minute, of every hour, of every day. It can process a half million options and possibilities in a few seconds. No wonder creativity is so easy for humans. All we have to do is learn to trust our marvelous brains and our subconscious and practice, practice,

practice. That will keep the ideas flowing! Creativity is as natural and necessary to humans as breathing.

Brenda Ueland said, "So you see, imagination needs noodling — long, inefficient, happy, idling, dawdling and puttering."

Chapter 10
Creativity and Change

"Change in all things is sweet." -
Aristotle

As life progresses, you will discover certain inescapable changes occurring. These include social changes all around you and involving you, as well as personal changes in your own life.

Creativity and change are closely related, and in fact, depend on one another. When change happens in your life, it takes creativity sometimes to get through it. Creativity then causes another change in how you respond to a given situation. Both the new change and the creativity to handle it have certain risks involved and will move you in a new direction. You may experience fear and anxiety; and at the same time, there may be joy and excitement.

Sometimes, these changes can occur too rapidly in a short span of time. The loss of much tradition in one's life and too much newness can cause a person to suffer, and can even lead to a nervous breakdown. There are certain limits to our ability to bounce back and recover from sudden changes. These things take time.

While we may experience strong motivation to certain changes and a determination to be accepting, there are also equally strong inhibitions against those same changes. Humans are contrary by nature.

Here are a few examples of the social changes that occurred between the years 1950 and 1980:

> • The percentage of married women who were wage earners, with children under the age of six, went from 12% to 45%.
> • In 1950, only one child in ten did not live with both parents. By 1980, it was one child in four.
> • Between 1950 and 1980, the divorce rate doubled.
> • The proportion of men in the labor force over the age of sixty-five fell by more than half.

You can easily see where changes of this magnitude would require some very creative solutions for all those involved, as well as their families. But change happens; it's just a part of living. Life is just one change after another, but that's what helps us to grow and develop as humans. It only makes it harder for you if you fight change.

There are also personal changes that require a great deal of creativity to make it through. Marriage is a change that demands a certain amount of creativity. Adjustments of all kinds are needed here, starting with where to live, money issues, family issues (hers and his), and schedules.

Having children is another huge change that must be dealt with every day by many people. The need for creativity here is equally huge. Caring for another human being requires real inspiration. Then once again, there are adjustments needed, such as providing for a family, aside from money issues, schedules, and family issues. Women especially have to be highly creative to deal with the problems these life changes bring about, since they are often in charge of most of the above-mentioned issues. Of course, single motherhood brings with it a whole new set of problems to be solved as creatively as possible for everyone involved.

The sudden loss of a spouse is another personal change that is very difficult to deal with and requires a great deal of creativity to get through. At this time, it is often necessary not only to make a change. It is equally important to re-evaluate your entire life; and in effect, re-invent yourself and your priorities. Creativity is absolutely the key to making it through this particular trauma. Re-invention of self on a daily basis is essential.

Loss of a job or a home is enough to send many people into a spiral of depression and hopelessness. Real creativity is needed here to turn the situation around to your advantage. You can choose to move elsewhere. If you lose your job, you can find another, or you can start your own business.

Change brings with it an opportunity. You can go with it, or play the victim and feel sorry for yourself.

It's often said that necessity is the mother of invention. Many great insights, discoveries, and novel inventions have come about because their creators were in desperate need. They turned to their own individual creativity for resolution.

> Henri Bergson said, "To exist is to change, to change is to mature, to mature is to go on creating oneself endlessly."

Like it or not, change will happen to you. And once you realized that change is inevitable and should not be feared, you're ahead of the game. Maybe a major life change has happened to you already, maybe not. But you can't avoid it. In fact, it's actually easier if you try and embrace the change, rather than rail against it. This is a place where you can use your creativity to your best advantage.

Whether it's getting married, starting a family, losing a job, finding a new job, starting your own business, or any other change wreaking havoc in your life, creativity is the key to success. Go back to the creative problem solving we've discussed earlier, take a deep breath, and plunge right in. We've all been there, or will be eventually. It's not what happens to you in life that's important. It's how you handle those events that matter; it's how you allow your creative side to deal with the problems that count.

Adam R. Gwizdala said, "Everything in life changes you in some way. Even the smallest things. If you do not accept these changes, you do not accept yourself. For through these changes brings new and greater things to you, making you wiser, as time progresses. To avoid these changes is a loss. You only live your life once. Do not waste a minute of it avoiding things. Let them come to you, and learn from them. There is always tomorrow."

In addition, George Bernard Shaw said,
"Life isn't about finding yourself. Life is
about creating yourself."

Chapter 11
Baby Boomers & Creativity

"Do not seek to follow in the footsteps of the men of old; seek what they sought."
– Basho

More than seventy-six million people in the United States are currently feeling a major change. That would be the Baby Boomers, and they are the most powerful demographic in history. This represents the largest single sustained growth of the population in the nation's history.

It also represents the largest group of creative people all alive and kicking - making music, writing books, buying and selling, and helping others.

In a previous chapter, we discussed the fact that your brain is gathering and processing information all the time. Well, this group of people, collectively, has amassed an incredible amount of knowledge: facts, figures, images, ideas, words, and music, all in the course of fifty plus years.

As an example, we have Oprah Winfrey, who not only creatively designed her own production company, but also founded the Angel Network, making it possible for many young people to attend college and for philanthropic groups to continue their good works.

Another example of creativity from the Boomer generation would be Paul McCartney. He's been writing music and singing since the early sixties.

Stephen King has been writing short stories and novels since the late sixties, creatively showing us all how to be scared to death.

The list of stars over fifty, yet still showing us creativity on the big screen includes Michael Douglas, Diane Keaton, Sally Field, Tommy Lee Jones and Candace Bergen. Inspiring directors like Steven Spielberg continue to amaze us with such awesome display of talent and creativity.

But there is still plenty of room for all the rest of the not-so-famous-Baby Boomers to show us their creativity and their talent. With lifetime experiences to back them up, they are sure to amaze us. This generation will not be sitting on the porch or in their rocking chairs bemoaning the loss of the "good old days." They have a lot to draw on and a lot of creativity to share with us. They sing, they dance, they paint, and they write stories and music. They consult, and they teach. They pass along a long life's worth of experiences, images, sounds, ideas and inspiration.

The Japanese have a proverb that reads, "I will master something, and then the creativity will come." The Boomers have mastered many great skills and have developed many great talents. They have learned to recognize inspiration when they see or hear it, and they're responding to it. They're also sending it along to the next generation, continuing to inspire everyone.

Ray Bradbury once said, "We are all
cups, constantly and quietly being filled.
The trick is knowing how to tip ourselves
over and let the beautiful stuff out."

That is the trick. We have all been filled and continue to be filled with creative ideas and knowledge. We must let that creativity spill out, for our own sakes as well as for others.

Allow inspiration into your life and see what a difference it makes. Invite your Muse to stand close by and shower you with the necessary inspiration. If you put your mind to it (the left brain and the right brain), you will come up with all manners of creative ideas to deal with any aspects of your life.

No matter what difficulties arise, no matter what challenges you face, no matter what kind of roadblocks you encounter, your creativity will help you to overcome all of them. Go back to your childhood, when your teacher told all of you to put on your thinking caps. Try it on for size now, you may discover it still fits.

There's nothing like inspiration to help you conquer your fears. It will change your life, guaranteed. Let go of the past and its disappointments; they only trip you up and hold you back.

Make use of every source to aid you in this quest for creativity. Inspiration is all around you. The basic desire is within you; the need for creativity is a part of your very DNA. You simply have to train your brain to think more creatively, allow that desire to fill you, and force that creativity to the surface. You may have to remind yourself each and every day to think creatively, give yourself the chance to come with a bit of inspiration of your own, and find ways to solve your problems. You may even discover inside yourself an artist, a writer, a musician, or an inventor struggling to get out. Let the creative spirit inside of you come out to play, and create.

If you find the need for a little more inspiration, talk with Baby Boomers about what thrills them. See if it's something you might like to try. Then get them to teach you all about it. Read a book, take a class, and learn to play an instrument or dance. Contact your local Continuing Education Center and find out what kinds of creative activities you can engage in.

John W. Gardner tells a story of Alexander the Great visiting Diogenes. Alexander asked whether he could do anything for the famed teacher. Diogenes replied, "Only stand out of my light." Gardner concluded that perhaps some day, we should know how to heighten creativity. Until then, one of the best things we can do for creative men and women is to stand out of their light.

Perhaps we should stand close enough to that light, to shed a little beam on us, for us to learn from those creative men and women. Then we can go out and share a little of that light to others. We can help pass the torch to the next generation.

Chapter 12
Zen and the Art of Creative Maintenance

"Zen is not some kind of excitement, but concentration on our usual every day routine" - Shunryu Suzuki

To achieve a Zen-like state, everything needs to be in alignment. Harmony is the key word. The problem is there in front of you, along with the necessary skills and talent. You know you can do it. You're filled with self-confidence. Creative energy fills the room. Everything just clicks. It's the perfect atmosphere for problem solving. And the more people involved in the process, the more energy there is.

When the creative energy is in full force and you know your skills are matched perfectly with the task, it's known as the "white moment." It's a moment when everything fits together harmoniously. Athletes refer to it as being "in the zone." They can't do anything wrong. Their skills are so well matched to the challenge, they almost blend together.

In the scientific world, this is known as "the flow." It doesn't matter what activity you apply it to; if the skills meet the challenge, you are filled with that creative energy. The air almost crackles with that creative electricity. The ideas are flowing and everything is working in perfect harmony. What you're doing seems unified and almost feels effortless. You feel as if you could do it in your sleep.

You can tell that it's not right if your talents and skills are not up to the task. You will feel anxious and more fearful of failure. If by some chance, your skills far surpass the challenge at hand, you'll become bored and restless. At this point, you're simply not using your skills to your best advantage. You need more of a challenge.

Neurologists have determined that while you're in "the flow," you actually expend less energy than you do when you're wrestling with the original problem.

That's because the necessary skills for the task at hand are at the surface and readily available to you, while those skills not necessary at the moment are relatively silent. When you're feeling anxious or confused, there's basically no difference in the energy exerted.

When you're in that state of "flow," you lose all sense of time, or self-consciousness. In the Zen philosophy, this is called **no-mind**. You become so absorbed in what you're doing, you actually become lost in the project. This is when you've tapped into the greater creative energy to which you have access.

Children are more likely to enter that "flow" state than adults. They simply can lose themselves and forget about time. Adults are more conscious of the passage of time than children, who are more comfortable in this "timeless state."

What's frustrating for children is to be ripped out and jerked back into the rigid clock-driven society when they are completely absorbed in that timeless state of creativity. Too much scheduling can stifle the creativity of a child. Indeed, it can stifle the creativity of any of us. John Bradshaw said, "Children are natural Zen masters; their world is brand new each and every day."

What we all need is more Zen no-mind time to indulge in whatever creative pursuits we fancy. We need to create a more Zen-like atmosphere at work and at home. Nothing is more energizing than being in the "zone," the "white moment," or the "flow." Try to find moments when you can slip out of time and in to a more Zen-like state of no-mind. Enjoy your project. Enjoy solving that problem and putting it behind you.

Now off you go to the next creative endeavor. So many ideas, so little time!

Come to the edge
Life said.
We are afraid.
Come to the edge
Life said.
They came,
It pushed Them…
And
They
Flew!

- Guillaume Apollinaire

A SHORT piece about this book

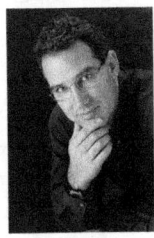 I have realized that a new path for my journey has arisen. God had blessed us richly. It is time to free myself from the yoke of the corporate world again and have the freedom that comes from working at home. No worry about finances, a time clock or traveling when it is not convenient for the family.

The Astonishing Secret That Will Set You Free ...
I have been a student of personal development and wealth creation for 20 years. I have searched various enterprises and hundreds of business opportunities. I have tried dozens, succeeded at some and failed miserably at many. There are some things I have found to be extremely important, (**actually absoutely critical**), to abundance creation.
How would you like to harness the awesome mental magic that lies latent within your own mind?
Who would you become, if you could suddenly unleash herculean confidence in your own abilities?
What riches await you, if you could unlock your creative imagination to attract unbridled success?
The secret is in plain sight. Yet ONLY THOSE WHO ARE READY and SEARCHING FOR IT will find it.

If you are READY to put it to use, you will recognize this secret.

I wish I could tell you how you will know if you are ready, but that would deprive you of much of the benefit you will receive when you make the discovery in your own way.

A peculiar thing about this secret is that those who acquire it and use it find themselves literally swept on to success, with little effort, and they never again submit to failure!

The secret serves all who are ready for it equally well. Education has nothing to do with it. Money has nothing to do with it. Connections have nothing to do with it.

ALL in possession of the secret need only reach out and avail themselves of all the abundance and happiness they desire.

Somewhere as you read, the secret will jump from the page and stand boldly before you, IF YOU ARE READY FOR IT!

THANK YOU!

I appreciate you visiting our website and your continued support of our blogs and websites. You can find free resources visiting
http://www.mamarazziguides.com.

Godspeed.

Books Available

As a Man Thinketh

Mamarazzi Guides (2011)

Acres of Diamonds

DISCLAIMER AND TERMS OF USE AGREEMENT

The author and publisher have used their best efforts in preparing this report. The author and publisher make no representation or warranties with respect to the accuracy, applicability, fitness, or completeness of the contents of this report. The information contained in this report is strictly for educational purposes. Therefore, if you wish to apply ideas contained in this report, you are taking full responsibility for your actions.

EVERY EFFORT HAS BEEN MADE TO ACCURATELY REPRESENT THIS PRODUCT AND IT'S POTENTIAL. HOWEVER, THERE IS NO GUARANTEE THAT YOU WILL IMPROVE IN ANY WAY USING THE TECHNIQUES AND IDEAS IN THESE MATERIALS. EXAMPLES IN THESE MATERIALS ARE NOT TO BE INTERPRETED AS A PROMISE OR GUARANTEE OF ANYTHING. SELF-HELP AND IMPROVEMENT POTENTIAL IS ENTIRELY DEPENDENT ON THE PERSON USING OUR PRODUCT, IDEAS AND TECHNIQUES.

YOUR LEVEL OF IMPROVEMENT IN ATTAINING THE RESULTS CLAIMED IN OUR MATERIALS DEPENDS ON THE TIME YOU DEVOTE TO THE PROGRAM, IDEAS AND TECHNIQUES MENTIONED, KNOWLEDGE AND VARIOUS SKILLS. SINCE THESE FACTORS DIFFER ACCORDING TO INDIVIDUALS, WE CANNOT GUARANTEE YOUR SUCCESS OR IMPROVEMENT LEVEL. NOR ARE WE RESPONSIBLE FOR ANY OF YOUR ACTIONS.

MANY FACTORS WILL BE IMPORTANT IN DETERMINING YOUR ACTUAL RESULTS AND NO GUARANTEES ARE MADE THAT YOU WILL ACHIEVE RESULTS SIMILAR TO OURS OR

ANYBODY ELSE'S, IN FACT NO GUARANTEES ARE MADE
THAT YOU WILL ACHIEVE ANY RESULTS FROM OUR IDEAS
AND TECHNIQUES IN OUR MATERIAL.

The author and publisher disclaim any warranties (express or
implied), merchantability, or fitness for any particular purpose.
The author and publisher shall in no event be held liable to any
party for any direct, indirect, punitive, special, incidental or other
consequential damages arising directly or indirectly from any use
of this material, which is provided "as is", and without warranties.

As always, the advice of a competent professional should be
sought.

The author and publisher do not warrant the performance,
effectiveness or applicability of any sites listed or linked to in this
report.

All links are for information purposes only and are not warranted
for content, accuracy or any other implied or explicit purpose.

Thank You For Reading.

Part of the mission at Mamarazzi Guides is to reach out and help people design the life our creator intended for them. There are a ton of tools that we use to help make that happen. I am especially interested in mentoring and teaching in the area of stay at home business in art and photography, personal development in another area as realizing our individual potential begins there. The message contained in this book I believe can begin the transformation that can change lives, even save lives. I want to solicit your help in positively changing the status quo. The very important task that you can do is pass this book along, recommend it to anyone you know that may need a pick me up. What an amazing tool we have with the internet to affect change. With the click of a button you can send this book as a gift to anyone.

Thank-you,

Tim ONeill